Asperous

Art~~istry~~

KONDWANI FIDEL

ACKNOWLEDGMENTS

I would like to thank my two grandmothers, Mary Phoenix and Gail Russell. They both played a critical role in the process of building me into the iron-willed young man I am today. If it was not for the love of these two women, there would be no Kondwani Fidel. Without them, none of this would be possible.

Table of contents

- 2. Introduction
- 4. Anti-Poetry
- 8. The Child In Me
- 11. Seize The Start of Spring
- 13. Closed Mouths Don't Get Fed
- 17. Weeping
- 19. Elixir Love
- 25. The Wounded Bird
- 27. Soul Searching
- 30. Candy Savage
- 32. Mad For My Mate
- 35. The Writing Wrath
- 37. Misguided Guardians
- 44. Spiritual Warfare
- 46. My Unsolved Mysteries
- 49. Let's Take A Drthink
- 51. Remember
- 56. Don't Love Me
- 57. Tangible Turmoil
- 59. Why Did You Leave Me?
- 61. Trust the First Megabus
- 63. Unsung Prophecy
- 66. Where Is Everyone
- 68. Where I'm From
- 70. True Love
- 75. Corrosive Care
- 77. Destruction of Beauty
- 80. Best I Never Had
- 84. My Last Duchess
- 86. Freaky Dreams
- 90. Easy Route
- 92. I Yearn a Woman
- 95. The Minimal Moments
- 97. Bazaar
- 99. Bum
- 101. Autumn Crocus
- 103. The Black Jelly Bean
- 105. I Ball
- 107. Luzerne
- 110. The Hood Robin Hood
- 112. Couldn't Fathom a Title
- 115. Bad Decisions

117. Who Am I?
119. Get Away
122. Good Life
125. Mortal Immortal
128. My World
131. Can You See The Dignity In The Warrior?
133. Kondwani's Kreed
136. Call Me Crazy
139. Ugly Memories

Introduction

In this realm of life we all come from different backgrounds, experiences, and beliefs. Although we are all unique, our mere existence shares a common thread which is emotion. Whether we realize it or not, we are all put here on earth to fulfill a purpose greater than ourselves. I believe that connecting people through emotion will create unity amongst mankind. We as humans cannot simply exist alone, we must learn to effectively coexist together to create a better society. This philosophy brings me to the purpose of my very own existence.

I feel that my existence is relevant because I wake up every day with the desire to inspire others. This desire is facilitated through creating artwork that shoots directly to the soul and that can bring a scorching campfire to a blistering cold heart. Each and every last one of us is born with the ability of a genius, but it is our job to find what that ability is and apply it to our lives so we can pursue our passion. God places miracles and resources in the palms of our hands, so that they can be utilized and put to use for the greater good of mankind. There is a very thin line between fate and coincidence, and I believe that everything happens for a reason. Therefore what you are holding in your hands right now was brought to you by fate. Furthermore, what you are holding in your hand is more than just a book of poems. This book is the fuel that will help you ignite your deepest burning desires. Enjoy your journey!

To become great, you have to be able to see past and break traditional barriers
-Kondwani Fidel

Poetry is an artistic form of expression that has no boundaries or at least one doesn't know about any boundaries until they "break them". However, poetry involves feeling and it is intended to strike emotion, no matter if it is good or bad. Poetry comes from the heart and it is an expression of the human spirit. Poetry is a reflection of our imagination, our past, our present, and our future. Poetry strengthens and nourishes the brain.

Anti-Poetry
People are going to criticize me.
Even if you lack breath I will hear the slander.
Is it because my art shakes loose from Shakespearean Stanzas?
The Mary Shelly lifestyle was basic, I'm not on it
My bohemian style writings will slay y'all insignificant sonnets.
I'm mad, bad, and dangerous to know, like the modern day Lord George
But my hymns come from him.
The fire that I write is what The Lord forged.
Although I share the same zodiac as William Butler Yeats,
I Study his old Irish art, and then I crumble his piece.
I am the incineration of his Tragic Generation
I'm impatient and can't take any more foolish desperation.
I don't want the money like Shawn and Marlon Wayans
Just give me the light and recognition of Jane and Mark Twain.
The only Arnold I acknowledge,
Is the one who hung out with Gerald.
Not Matthew, just Gerald, Stinky, and Fat Harold.
One day can my words worth more than Wordsworth?
Or even Wadsworth?
But I'll continue to stay mellow,
So long my Longfellow.....

I will not be like John Keats, who was mainly known for
Working in the shadow of past poets.
My Tonka truck, no one will ever be able to tow it.
My potent poetry will peel off in its own lane or own plane

And it will perpetuate my name, and hopefully my most dreamt future of fame.
I am the wild child
I will be the greatest celebrity of my time like Oscar Wilde.
But I won't fall and become imprisoned for gross indecency.
Because unlike him, I will not be creeping around with my own sex, do you see?
Growing up in the jungle I was labeled with an unwanted stigma,
They labeled me as a crook.
Not knowing that one day I would be best known for my words
That strike the hearts hard like Rudyard Kipling when he wrote the jungle book.
My short fuse multiplied by the way I leave the pen abused
If Alive; I would've given Langston Hughes the blues.
I respect all of my beautiful females and their power
But in this world I will devour every metaphor, verb, and simile of
Sarah Flowers.
What is there in a broke Boy's Will but tragedies and man fears?
No real peers, just real tears.
They say it cost to be the boss,
Or to be the world's most beloved poet like Robert Frost.
Just because Edgar Allan Poe lost his flow in my birth place, I will not walk in his shoes, but I will sweep up his footprints
And create my own space.

Now if you listened closely to my words
You will see that this is a sick poet's antidote.
A lot of these men had the heart of a woman just like Maya Angelou.

If poetry gets you choked up then this is the tree and the rope.
If you thought poetry died then this is the coke and the hope
Of a fiend, with two dollars and no regrets or remorse on their sleeves
That's going to get high by any means.

The creativity of an adult comes from his or her childlike psyche that survived the mature cloudburst.

-Kondwani Fidel

When you are a child you experience the world much differently. Children are very original and they have their own thoughts and ideas. As a child, your mind is more open and you will ask any question that strikes your curiosity without a second thought. As a child we view every motion and color more vividly and every color seemed more alive. Kids wonder, Why is the grass green? Why is the sky blue? Why don't animal talks? Etc. Our eyes and ears took in the spectacle of life with outermost emotion. These are the many things that adults take for granted on a daily basis. As we get older, we tend to stop viewing things as they are and we view things based on opinion. While growing into adults our childlike spirit usually dies. In order to be creative you need to keep a large portion of your childlike spirit so when you digest information you can not only consume but you can create. You can turn everything you consume into something original.

The Child In Me

Sometimes when I speak, my words are so complex.
At other times you can smell my mother's titties on my breath.
My mind is almost completely open,
I entertain original ideas.
But the only real love I share is with my inner child, no one else cares.
My reflection in the mirror fills me with questions about the world.
It's probably the child in me that can't keep me with one girl
My eyes, knows (nose) and ears consume more knowledge,
Than any tractor trailer ever consumed mileage.
Every obstacle in life I try to turn it into a game.
Because if I didn't, my inner child would break loose from my soul, shackles, and chains
And leave me Stuck in the middle of this low down dirty game
My inner child is the one thing since birth that keeps me from turning insane.
My adult side is the gadfly, it picks at my brain.
We living in pain, going insane,
Stuck in this stupid feeble minded simple circular lane.
I retain my child inside of me, despite the pressures of adulthood.
My dimensional mind is active, that's what makes my inner thoughts good.
I have a constant feeling of connecting thoughts and Ideas
But remember this is poetry, who the fuck really cares?
Can I bring in a crowd of empty ears as big as Britney Spears?
People minds are shackled, stuck on Gilligan's Island.

I will never get comfortable; I'll change clothes if I don't like the stylist.
That means branching off to new brands, clothing in more knowledge
When You Wish Upon A Star you can become *N Sync with your recipe.
My child like soul is what usually gets the best of me.
My adult side statutory rapes my destiny.
What are child labor laws? Just bars, hindering us from flipping the page.
The Gerber baby in me will forever be in my heart caged,
Working for minimum wage.
This is the mark that marks me ultimately plagued.
My child like thoughts conceive high levels of sage.
Now that's what you call having kids at a young age.

The harsh reality of life is that nothing last forever.
-Kondwani Fidel

The spring time is like an addictive drug. I love it when I have it in the palm of my hand. I crave it the most at the end when it slips away from my fingertips right in front of my eyes.

Seize The Start Of Spring
Right after winter I get excited because spring is near.
Right before you know it, spring is here.
Fresh flowers with marvelous colors and expensive scents.
You are the beginning of Spring does that make sense?
I want to seize this moment because the break of spring is the most beautiful sight in the world.
Nobody cares for the close of spring because Just like childhood memories,
Freshness and newness begins to fade away.
EVERYTHING is gone;
All the stunning plants with their bright characteristics.

I saw you sprout; I remember when you had a few petals.
I want to see you blossom on forever.
God why can't I seize the spring time so together we can settle?
Now it is always next year when spring will rise again
But there will be new flowers which are prettier and that smell better.
They might even take me off my feet in different shoes.
But these flowers...
These other flowers.
Will NEVER be you.

While everyone else is chasing sheep,
you should be knitting a sweater.
-Kondwani Fidel

You should never worry about what others think of you. If someone can't understand your grind then that is ok. It is your vision not everyone else's, so you can't expect people to understand what God put YOU on this Earth to do. If you have a talent that you do not "feel comfortable" with expressing to the world, then you are not making God as happy as possible. Pursuing your passion is showing God that you appreciate him. Chase your dreams or chase death, because if you are not growing you are dying.

Closed Mouths Don't Get Fed

I can't recall as to why my entire life I was modest.
Not telling anyone that I was an artist,
Knowing damn well in that room I was working the hardest.
I would always think, how can I gather food for my family, so for a life time they could harvest?
I was forced out of the placenta with the heart of a warrior.
I'm warning ya.
Instead of playing in the streets, juggling dreams and pills
I should've been informing the world of my prodigious skill.
I was always shy with big dreams hoping that I could touch the sky.
Everyone always had their intentions on I.
Yes me, yes me.
I was startled
I wondered why everyone had all eyes on me like Makaveli.
Everyone in my family expects me to be the greatest.
They look for me to bring the cheese home so I could grade us.
It's harder because the disobedient streets pave us.
Growing up it was no light in my home because all the house did was shade us.
People still wonder how did a young boy bloom in a home filled with blow.
Just ironic as a junkie being sober with a room full of blow
And Magic Don Juan being faithful in a room full of hoes.
I always kept my mouth closed that's why I wasn't fed.
But we were always fed up with the feds disturbing our disturbed home looking for my mom and my dad.

Despite that irrelevance I have always been an artist and I have always worked my hardest.
All I had was my pen and paper on the shelf.
I never wrote my mom or dad while they were incarcerated because they melted my soul
These many words you all hear I could have been said them
But they were trapped inside a little boy who had trapped in him a little boy
And this little boy still cries for his mamma.
Where are you? Where are you Mamma?
Why are you hiding from me like I'm working for the government and you are Osama?
But I know you heard of karma, that bad bitch named karma.
She's going to eat your soul through all of your wool garments.
I should have been dropped my spoken words on the world like a comet
But I was too closed in and I was afraid that the bright lights would make me vomit.
Just the other day a man told me I looked very modest.
And he said closed mouths don't get fed and told me keep working my hardest.
Over and over he told me to stick to where my heart is.
Telling me this not knowing that I was an artist.
But his words stuck with me for a long time like how trees are stuck in the forest.
I'm the rose that sprouted from the concrete and my grandma was the florist.
Without her molding me into a man, I wouldn't be able to paint you this entire portrait.
A lot of the times I get mad because the words I'm spitting out like sunflower seeds I could have been said.
From now on I will never hush my mouth; I will never

be quiet
Like a glutton who is being forced on a diet.

*People are so focused on making their
outer identity glimmer,
not realizing that their inner man
is knocking on death's door.*
-Kondwani Fidel

    Crying can be one of the best feelings when something marvelous has happened in your life and you flood the Earth with tears of joy. You can be extremely happy because you are walking on the clouds and the air just taste so much better up there and you begin to cry. You can be in a relationship with someone you have a white-hot passion for and begin to cry because you never met anyone like him or her. Crying can also be one of the most inferior feelings that linger in the world. If a close relative dies you might cry tears of fire and hurt because you think of all the things you've done together, could've done together, or simply because the act of death causes great grief for many. The act of physical, emotional, and (or) mental distress can cause one to cry. Just because one cries, does not mean they always shed tears. Some cry and shed no tears because their many sorrows are internally caged away into a dry soul.

Weeping
I weep but shed no tears
No tears to be found,
Just my thoughts astounded with
The pain and the pressure people force on
You too look impressive.
If your physical or moral character doesn't
Make the cut for society's roll call.
Then they will outcast you in a corner and you will get stoned on a stone wall.
Now you are forced to brawl.
With whom you ask?
It's the you in the mirror,
But some people kill it hoping their vision
Becomes clearer.

Would you believe me if I said that I'm in love? I don't believe myself.
The red button I pushed, can you see I beg help?
-Kondwani Fidel

Love can be one of the scariest things in this world if you are in love with the wrong person or thing.

Elixir Love
I will love you forever baby please don't leave me.
Save your lies we got a love thing, I can tell that you need me.
They say that real love is never ever easy.
I want forever love; I'm tired of you trying to tease me.

I'm the only thing out here that's lethal and legal.
I've been around since medieval.
I'll roc your world fella, not talking about Beanie Sigel.
I know that having me in your life sometimes make things harder.
I must admit, I had relations with your grandfather.
Just to have me for a brief moment he would kill for loose dollars and quarters.
If I was only found in Mexico he would cross the border.
He killed himself fucking with me.
He knew that I would burn him to the 3rd degree.
Him too tried to leave, thought he had some tricks up his sleeve.
But he came back crawling.
One night kept calling
So I answered.
Then he came to see me, I had him all over the house falling.
After some months of not seeing me, he then kept me around for days.
And the end result left him six foot in the grave.
I'm a mean ass bitch, tougher than any boy or girl.
You have to be a real soldier to meddle in this world.

I will love you forever baby please don't leave me.
Save your lies we got a love thing, I can tell that you

need me.
They say that real love is never ever easy.
I want forever love; I'm tired of you trying to tease me.

Do you see how distraught you are when you try to live without me?
You can't leave me forever boy don't even try to doubt me.
YOU NEED ME BOY
I was there for you when nobody else was
Despite the mistakes I made, like when I started dating your cousins.
I'M YOUR SOULMATE, YOU TOLD ME I WAS YOUR SIGNIFICANT OTHER!
Who was there when you were sad about the death of your little brother?
Who took the pain away on that rainy day?
When you lacked money for them college funds you couldn't pay.
TELL ME WHO TOOK AWAY THAT MISERY!?
When you were alone, you use to always visit me.
Now the word around town is you creeping with Mani?
She's nothing more than a weak bitch
What you can't handle this, all of this G shit?
I was there when you took your first shot; I remember how it treated your lips.
I know sometimes I'm hard to deal with.
Especially after you've been hooked for years.
If you ever decided to leave me for another
When you find your baby mother,
I'm going right after your kids.
I was there when your last girl cheated
When your heart was blistering cold, when you were real heated.
Who were you thinking about when you were locked down in that cell?

Me boy! I'm where all of your thoughts dwell.
When I'm not around you crave me.
Saying to yourself "baby please come save me.
From all of this confusion and pain.
I need you to keep me sane.
You are not like the others baby your completely insane.
Your love is like poison, you are the taste of love like sautéed tilapia soaked in hoison"
Sometimes I nibbled at your liver,
I would be you Jeffrey Dahmer
But that's in the past I promise you baby, no more drama.
You tried to leave me, because you was afraid of what people was thinking.
Why are they in your business watching where you are winking?
All up in your cup, tell them don't worry about what you are drinking.

I will love you forever baby please don't leave me.
Save your lies we got a love thing, I can tell that you need me.
They say that real love is never ever easy.
I want forever love; I'm tired of you trying to tease me.

I know this love is real because baby your still here.
After all of those long nights when I slept with your peers.
I made Edgar Allan Poe drop dead in your birth place.
Lenore had nothing on me; he got it in the worse way.
I use to sex Johnny cash.
I had Johnny down bad.
Bon Scott to, he overdosed on me raw.
And I left his ass in his car just to "sleep the pain off"
You know I'm bisexual, Billie Holiday even swallowed me.

I ate that little girl alive.
She wasn't really ready for me, ready for the ride.
I can't believe you haven't seen all of those movies I starred in.
I even had that sexy white woman Judy Garland.
I dealt with so many celebrities; boy you know that I'm true.
You should be excited that I'm even messing with you!!!
I want you to be with me forever I don't care what your friends say.
I lay with you on late nights and throughout the day.
When you're so called "bottom chick" wasn't there to go all the way down and take you to the top.
I came running boy and I made your imagination rock.
You tried to tell me that I was darkness, and I had no lighting.
On several occasions I triggered that light bulb in your head and influenced your writing.
When I'm not around your friends call me a gold digger.
But I still messed with you, even when you couldn't afford Snickers.
I let you hold your little funds tight, you was on your Yom Kippur.
I didn't forget that night when you spent my money to tip strippers.
Everybody know not to talk dirty when I come around.
Because when I get in your system they know we shutting the party down.
I thought this was love but you are trying to creep out and leave me.
I ain't stupid boy I see you, I'm not Stevie.

Promise me that a few more times you'll take me home.
Even if you have to steal and sell your granny's

Iphone.
I make your vision blurry, but please try to see me.
Just one last time, even if you have to steal your grandmother's TV.
If you ever decide to visit me, just let me know when.
Boy don't act like you don't know where I be.
Monday through Sunday late nights, I'm on every other corner posted
Out here till 3.

> *Never let anyone see that*
> *your shoes are too small.*
> *Always stand strong*
> *even if your toes are balled up.*
> *He who buries his struggles in the sand*
> *shall find gold.*
> *-Kondwani Fidel*

Even when you are lacking, never let your enemy see it. If you are a person that wear feelings and problems on your sleeves. Make sure you wear it well and make it look good. No matter how hard life gets, fight through any and every battle. How many times you fall and then get back up is how your success will be measured. You become stronger and more resilient as you grow.

The Wounded Bird
Although the bird smiles, hope dangles on a string.
You can hear the pain and misery whenever the bird sings.
To God it sounds beautiful
To others it is an ugly scream.
The fully feathered birds try to clip the wounded bird's wings.
So is it not hard for the bird to fly and clutch his dreams?
Will this bird receive its blessing?
Try flying a little harder so you won't leave your mind guessing.
Fly bird fly!
God has faith in you, why?
Because God seen many wingless birds fly and embrace the sky.
Sometimes God sticks his strongest soldiers in the most powerless disguise.

I will never auction my soul.
I will never bargain my brain.
I will never sell off my goals.
I will forever hawk over my name.
					-Kondwani Fidel

    One of the hardest tasks in life is for people to find them true selves. Many people end up not taking the time out of their life to find who they truly are and end up dressing up like another up until they die. Don't do things for the wrong reason, or live life as someone else and not yourself. If you do, no matter how much success you think you have faced; once you reach the end of your life you will see that it was a misadventure.

Soul Searching
All I do is search high and low every day
To find a me,
A me that doesn't yet exist.
So all I'm doing is beating me up with a closed anxious filled fist.
But in my mind I have a list
Which was something I thought quick
It was simple and handpicked and went something like this.
Can I take a bath in the ocean with the bizarre Baptist?
And sea how bad and sad the wrath gets?
Can I see how much sick dick a trick can take if she's Catholic?
Some females come up with logistics just to get dicks.
I got off topic,
That's something I want to change.
When I write, I can never stay in my own lane.
The Kondwani that I want, I have to make grow.
This is not the little Koni I knew a few years ago.
Never did I think it would get this difficult.

When people ask for help and you cut em a slice of the fritter
If it's not as big as they want it, they will still act bitter.
My mind is like a harvest and every day I plant successful seeds.
My drive to help mankind is what Adam Sandler my Mr. Good Deeds.
I need patience, because if you want your harvest too soon then it's going to die out.
And the fruits of your labor will fly out
All of your cabbage will decay.

So just take every twenty four hours day by day.
Failures will make you great,
So that means I have to fail soon.
Or my hunger for success will be my ultimate crowned doom.
So if you have a deep rooted passion, you better be able to withstand failures and setbacks.
Ignore the doubters and critics.
Also ignore the stigmatisms of the belligerent wack bitches.
So get through your final days of drudgery.
And instead of chasing the chicks, substitute the chicks for ways to get rich.
So you can hunt down The Great White Whale Moby Dick.

Give me a reason why you shouldn't assume that everyone is against you.
-Kondwani Fidel

    Only give people what you want them to know. Think of life as a chess game; are you going to tell your opponent your next move if you are trying to win? I don't think so. When a terrorist is planning an attack do they announce when they are going to do so? I think not. Always be unpredictable, make sure that every idea and motion you are about to bring forth is hanging by a thread so no one, I mean no one knows what direction you will swing. Don't let others prepare for what you are getting ready to do. You do let them get a feeling that a storm is coming, but that is ok because they still will not know how strong the winds are.

Candy Savage
The clouds look like cotton candy, for the candy I thirst
So I'm shooting for the skies so I can let the starburst.
I wake up every morning with a drive to write
To become much more potent
Y'all can have the ice, just give me the light.

Lately my bright future has been eying me and trying me.
God wants me to be great in this society that lies to me.
My thoughts are unmarked jewels trapped in a chamber
With signs that barricade, "enter at your own risk & may cause danger".
My thoughts scramble like Randall and they always get the best of me.
I have an urge to chase what's left of my destiny
Even if this race of life takes the last breath from me.
Gaining these unmarked jewels can lead to a world of trouble.
If they are filled with life or death, I'm still going to hustle.
In order to feel the pain you have to go through your own struggles.
Manifest some dreams to snuggle.
Clutch some dreams then smuggle.
And share them with nobody because nobody really loves you.
Nobody really loves you.

> *When I have writers block*
> *I think of you, because I hope the*
> *thoughts of you*
> *will make my work as beautiful too.*
> *-Kondwani Fidel*

    When a good man is searching for a good woman, a man is searching for meaning and value. He is searching for something out of this world; something that's way beyond the nine planets. Women are the most beautiful creatures on Earth. They are more precious than any jewel, and more valuable than any material.

Mad For My Mate
When I think of two people loving, I never think we.
Could I someday be that husband loved by a wife-ee?
Would she be happy with the man I am becoming?
Or will she keep dwelling in my past, so just Like
Edgar Allan Poe
All I keep hearing is the black Raven whining its
mourning sing.

I want the love that Oceans KONnot quench.
My popular demand for love
I'm the free agent, just waiting to be picked up off the
bench.

Yes I have buried a few females' hearts into a trench.
But to God this is my plea, this is as real as it will get.
Sometimes the stench of love really gets me sick
Whenever I think about all the girls who clutch a bag
filled with Magic's tricks.

I just want her to prize my love more than the bricks
of gold that
the government holds.
My ultimate goal is that before I die to make sure you
stitch this black hole.
No matter the circumstances I never want you to fold
and die by my side,
While our hairs turn gray and our bones crawl cold.

I want us to make love in the sky, and you can scream
proud
I could care less how loud.
The flames that we ignite will split holes through the
clouds
That will reach Earth's surface
Then smash into the cement, which will make the fire
ooze through the cracks In the ground.

Making the devil sick of sin, saying that he wish he would've stayed an angel somehow.

> *My mind constantly moves.*
> *My moves are constantly constant.*
> *My constant flux of ideas flow with proper precaution.*
> *-Kondwani Fidel*

    My mind is my slut. I let my mind get seduced by any and every idea that catches my attention. I mingle with these ideas until a much better one comes along. I have a kind of sexual excitement for ideas which keeps my mind on the move. On the other hand I write because it is what I love to do. The only time I don't love to write is when it is forced, for example having to write a paper in school. I write when I feel like my heart needs it, which just happens to be every day. Whenever I get inspired I write, and almost anything inspires me. I tend to use double meanings in almost all of my work and it's great if people can understand and catch the double meaning. If not, I'm still happy as a writer because I was able to challenge myself and then conquer. I am fascinated with looking up new words and finding out the meaning so I can have sort of a challenge when it comes to one of my future pieces which I will find a creative way to use the word. I also write for others, hoping that there is someone out there who can relate. Maybe some of my work can help a person get through their day because of the inspiration I embark upon. It's amazing when someone can relate to my deepest darkest emotions and secrets.

The Writing Wrath
It's never hard to write, even about what I don't know.
Sometimes I try my hardest, sometimes I try my least.
Whenever I write about my childhood
I'll always break you off just a little piece.
A piece of what is supposed to be light.
But it is forever dark like a bat cave.
I remember crawling up that beaten down staircase.
When I was close to the top of that beaten set of stairs.
I had my face spat in, I was filled with despair.

It's society's biggest bull's eye.
They crush drugs, they keep it stable.
The Caine was always Abel
To bully its way onto my dirty kitchen table
Which disabled my cable, my cartoons, and my mother's spiritual label.

Crawling up the steps, may I speak for all?
I'd love to.
The higher you are, the harder you'll fall.
Just look at what my crooked crayon draws.

The pilots who landed my plane were pretty high.
God is the biggest drug addict in the sky.
The clouds are bags of cocaine passing by.

> *Why spend a lifetime trying to repair dysfunctional men and women when it's much easier to build strong kids.*
> *-Kondwani Fidel*

    The reason behind the many children who are not positive products of their society is the parents. Parents are not parenting anymore. A parent is their child's first teacher; therefore the child learns from the parent directly and indirectly through actions and words. Many of these parents teach their children all of the wrong things then are baffled when their child grows up on the wrong path becoming products of their evil environment. In my neighborhood and many other ghetto areas there are not enough fathers in the households to help out the women with raising kids. In the same breath, there are many men who are in their children's lives but they are weak. These men let their child do whatever they want, say whatever they want, and get away with it. So what good is it if the man is present but is too weak to take control and run his home? It's just as equivalent to a father not being there. So that extra void that is missing gets filled in by many other negative influences which lead the child to failure. Therefore; people need to have better decision making when it comes to the person they choose to have a child with. Parents need to do a better job at raising their children and be more of a parent than a friend. Teach your child morals and values that will help them positively progress through life.

The Misguided Guardians
Let's take a trip to Baltimore, lets hop in the time machine.
Close your eyes and let me tell you about this young gamine.
She was just a young teen, her name was Jazneen.
Slim waist with pretty eyes, nice face and her ass was mean
But the only thing is she's only nineteen.
On her third abortion,
Because of her good charm the naked eye never seen,
All the babies that was killed by Jazneen.
She must work for the clinic
Because her mouth has seen more tools then dentist.
Why majority of young females put up their pussy for sale?
Free of charge
We all know The Heart Is Not So Smart like El DeBarge.
Jazneen's mother was never there, she never taught her about that time of the month,
Never put barrettes in her hair.
How is a girl supposed to move when her mother never cared?
How is a girl supposed to act when all she sees is her mother letting numerous dudes sex her wild and pull her hair?
You know what they say about a parent who has a child but doesn't want to pay the cost.
Guess what?
The child lost.

Jazneen runs around the hood with her panties on fire.
She loves chasing Instagram and the men she desire.
Jazneen is sleeping with Tay, David and Little Sean.
Tay just loves to get high, David he's the good guy
And little Sean is really little, he just finished junior

high.

Jazneen awakes one morning throwing her lungs up.
Everyone is in love with the fast lane until they crash, this life sucks.
She doesn't tell her mother because their relationship is detached.
Her mother only cares about talking greasy while in the club making her butt clap.
So Jazneen goes alone to visit the doctor.
He has some good and bad news
So she says "please doc read me the reviews"
The doctor lays down the good and say "you are not dying, that's the best segment
I'm not the smartest man in the world, but Jazneen your pregnant"

She let the doctor explain nothing more, she jets out the front door crying and asking "why lord?"
Jazneen is so scared; her body can't withstand another abortion.
She already killed 3 kids.
Since David is the good guy she prays the baby is his.
But remember she is also sleeping with Tay and little Sean
Different days, no rubbers, from dusk till dawn.
She tells Tay "I'm pregnant baby what we gonna do"?
Tay rebuttals "don't say baby in the same sentence with me and you"
Remember Tay get high so all he worry about is grass,
All he care about is his sales and where to place his stash.

So later she sees little Sean and say "I have to tell you something"
Sean seen the scared look in her eyes, and knew she was about to say a whole bunch of nothing.

Sean acts nonchalant and say "what the fuck you want"?
Jazneen say "baby I think we have one on the way"
He said "what a hurricane? Get the hell out my face"
She says "no baby please don't act shady.
You said you would love me no matter what, and I'll forever be your lady"

Sean says, "what? You not my lady, you know we been done?
Plus you already know I got a 1 year old son.
It can't be mine I remember using condoms when I was fucking you fast"
What is Sean going to do with another baby?
He can barely wipe his own ass.

The young gamine is flustered with confusion.
Don't start up the game if you don't know how to play it.
She is sitting down and she calls David.
David said "what's up baby, how have you been?"
She says "Baby I need you bad, we really are deep in....
David you are the only person I have been sleeping with, and baby I'm pregnant"
David is so naive; he thought this was a phone call from Heaven.
So David asked not one thing.
He said "I love you and our child forever
Y'all won't have to ever worry about nothing"

David is so happy, David is such a lame.
Hours haven't even past, he's buying baby clothes and thinking about names.
Fast forward 9 months later
Little David is here, by God's grace.
I'm going to keep it to myself but David and his son don't really share the same face.
But you know you can't really tell when a child is an

infant.
So maybe I could be wrong.
But we know Jazneen was out pimpin.
David knows for sure Jazneen wasn't a whore.
So I'm going to save y'all sometime and fast forward a little more.

13 years later, little David he grows up.
Little hair on his nuts but he's still a young pup.
Jazneen is still hoeing? I didn't even have to ask it.
And his father is so simple he can't separate paper from plastic.
So who teaches the son? Take a guess
It's the streets.
The boy is only 13; his waist eternally burns from the heat.
Little David has no guidance.
His entire life, he was influenced by gangster music.
He would ride around in a stolen car, smoking weed, just nodding to it.
Waiting for someone to get out of pocket like a knife in a food fight.
David was a lone soldier with no parents he has been fighting all his life.
David turns the corner and he almost hit a guy who was crossing the street.
The boy looks at David and say "You non-driving bitch, do you see me crossing the street"?
David said "I'm in the right, you stupid ass is in the wrong"
Two stubborn angry kids, they could be fussing all night long.
The kid doesn't know that David is about to get in his ass like a thong.
The kid is thinking he can't be beat,
So he is steady talking trash.
Not knowing that little David has his thirty eight heat in arms reach.

David hops out of the car, aims his gun at the kid.
The kid looks scared so he stands there with a blank look as he scratches his hairless beard.

Flashback, Remember the bad news Jazneen never received from her doctor
Because she ran out the hospital drenched with rage?
The other news was that Jazneen had Aids.
However; little David too was born with the bug.
Fast forward, So that played a large role as to why David turned out to be a thug.
He felt as though he was a cursed child who was born in the mud.
David had nothing to lose, because he was born with Aids.
He feels like life isn't fair and a spade is a spade.
You can see that little David is maybe a year or two younger than the little kid
He still was around his age.
A year isn't a big difference so they held the same sage.
He told the boy "put your hands up before I kill you"
The boy hesitated and he went ahead and listened.
The boy stood there in shock, thinking "damn we look alike
We got the same face, same eyes, and we the same height"
The kid would have never hesitated if David was any other,
Because when he looked at David he saw the features of a twin brother.

So as the boy has his hands up, he thinks to himself "wait a minute, I'm not a chump,
So he reaches for his gun, and David shoots him and left him slumped.
Little David Blasted 3 shots into his kin out of his gun.

Little David didn't know but he killed his father's oldest son.

> *Pay attention, and Sea the Hawks*
> *like Seattle and victory will never be in doubt.*
> *Not in a hundred battles*
> *-Kondwani Fidel*

    Being at war with yourself can be one of the most dangerous wars of all time. It is more treacherous than a war with your enemy. This war is just a battle within you between two different parts of your soul. We all are Gemini, don't let anyone ever tell you differently. However; on one side you have hate, self-doubt, and ego. On the other side you have love, hope, and truth. If you win then you win. If you lose, then I guess you just lose. The side of you that will win is the side that you nourish.

Spiritual Warfare
I'm scared to let people get close
Because my heart bares a hole.
It feels like I'm at war with my own disembodied soul.
So how do I win if I'm at war with myself?
I blame those 2 they should be ashamed of themselves.
The pain,
The pressure.
The beatings,
The whelps.
The rain,
The dark skies,
The cards I was dealt.
Do you feel my pain now?
Can you see I need help?
The pitch black nights,
They sicken my insides; can you see I need health?
My eyes are filled with desires; can you see I crave wealth?
I wake up every morning and I go through this routine
Of this young man fighting this war that's obscene.
This bloody war, forever on it goes.
I grab the gun and look at my heart
Damn there goes another hole.

> *No matter how much bad a person does,*
> *everyone has some righteousness in them.*
> *Even murderers*
> *say their grace before they eat*
> *-Kondwani Fidel*

    One thing you have to learn is that you grow through life and not just simply go through life. There are many bad things that we do as human beings but never see the real problem until we grow as people and look at the situation in hindsight. Have you ever done something that seems unlikely for your character, but you could not put your finger on as to why you did those things? Just believe that all of your actions (good or bad), blessings, and struggles are placed into your life for a reason.

My Unsolved Mysteries
Another broken heart on my hands.
Did anyone see me, where is the murder witness?
Check my sheet I have so many murder victims.
I look at my hand and say to myself "do you carry the murder mitten"?
Since you was young you've been breaking hearts with no discretion
And quick to ask God for some forgiveness.
Then I ask myself "would you harm another female"?
I don't even trust myself, therefore; I can't reveal any further details.
My insecure thoughts are what prevail
Me loving a good woman wholeheartedly, my plea fails.
When I was a young kin, sin would breeze through my wind.
Now I have a face like a devil sick of sin.

I didn't mean to hurt you
Maybe I really did, or maybe I just wanted to flirt you.
But not really drag you all through the dirt to hurt and desert you.
I didn't mean to give you temporary love like a 4:00am TV commercial.
It's my fault
I think I'm infected with D' evils.
Can't shake this feeling off
Where are you God? I NEED YOU!
You know I don't welcome myself in them awfully pretty cathedrals.
So this letter is one of the few ways I can talk to you.
I know I'm wrong Lord and I really want to get better.
But with my blind eyes I'm reading this letter
With these same blind eyes, can my pillows get any wetter?
Would if for the true love of a friend

I Paid in Full till the end?
Will I gain and hurt a friend ever again?
If Rico had the chance would he put on his Murder Mitten and kill Mich-i-gan?

Respect the dominion of your thoughts
-Kondwani Fidel

    Your thoughts control many of your actions believe it or not. Whatever consumes your mind controls your life.

Let's Take A Drthink
Every time I begin thinking about drinking.
I then try my hardest to layoff thinking about thinking.
Sometimes I do it to keep myself busy.
So I don't have to worry about where is she.

I've been baptized in a Bacardi beck.
I'm losing this race in a Rum river.
I choke the goose by its neck,
And then I annihilate it, like I have an immortal liver.
Whenever I ought to clear my mind.
Whenever I can't see,
I strap up my goggles and doggy paddle
In the Black Hennuh -Sea.

A young boy who drowns
Let me tell it,
Hearing him gasp for air, it's the best horrible sound.
Drinking, I tell you boy it's a really bad habit.
My True friends always tell me "boy you can't have it"
I try to break loose from the devil's liquid chain.
Sometime this makes me forget my aim,
Boy oh boy sometimes I fail to remember my name.

Sometimes I begin to think which keeps me sane.
Then I think about drinking, I claim it washes away the pain.
I sometimes validate drinking by saying I'm in college and it's a part of the game.

*How could one not remember
a time that was life changing?*
-Kondwani Fidel

    Most of my work comes from real life situations. Halloween comes more than once a year for many due to the masks they wear frequently. I'm sure many of us have experienced abandonment some time in our lives, if it was from a close friend or a relative. No matter how much a person forgives, none of us forgets; we will always remember.

Remember
Remember, once upon a time your love patched up all of my soars.
Then you ripped them back open when you abruptly said
"We can't do this anymore, we have to close all doors"
I thought we was together forever like college room and board
But you took all of your things and left me stranded on campus.
You branded my heart and left ashes, cut it all up and left gashes
Left me with wet eye lashes.
You had me thinking this life we could master
But you couldn't even receive bachelors.

You're no longer my Sun, no longer my Nash.
You were never my love, just hate wearing love's mask.

Failures will make you great, so if you lack experience that means you have to fail soon.
-Kondwani Fidel

We all have past experiences, some that we regret and some we appreciate. One makes bad decisions when they are unconscious of their moves, and more so unconscious of how extreme the result can be. When you speak of love, love is one of those things that usually get generalized by people from other peoples' past experiences. Love is an anomaly for many who don't ever care to study love, but tend to throw the word around so loosely. Many of us never take the time to turn ourselves into detectives and search for the real meaning of love. We never put love onto a platter and just dissect it, so we can catch sight of why we love love or why we hate love. Before anyone of us gain love from another, we have to first love ourselves. You have to look directly through the mirror, into your own eyes, look much deeper than your darkest pain, look into your own soul and find your true essence and discover who you are and what your life task is. Then you will find yourself smiling all the way home while marching up a miraculous road made out of milk and honey destined toward your lover and your success which are your true desires in life.

Don't Love Me
From day one you heard that I was not worth a dime or a damn.
The rumors and lies is what I was drenched in.
I take it back some things were the truth
Sometimes I could get downright ugly.
That is why I indirectly tell females please don't love me.

Once upon a time
I had sex with 2 friends; blood wouldn't have made them any closer
Not being attentive
Not knowing that karma is gonna getcha.
The lust was calling and me I kept falling
They saw it in my eyes; they knew the shots I was calling
I laid down the traps and like mice they came crawling
Few weeks later on the phone they were teary eyed balling.
I was ruthless
They wondered to themselves how could they be so stupid.
But they knew what they were dealing with from the start
She cut the caution tape and got their friendship ripped apart.
They knew I was bad news, hung in a bad crew
They knew I had a cold heart they knew that it was blue
But I think they loved me because they knew what was true
They knew I had potential, if my maturity grew.
At the end of the day, it cannot be any me and you
Don't love me...

Through all this bad I still have a good side I should

say
Remember I came on Lakewood and brought you flowers on your birthday?
I only adored you because of the potential I saw
Brainless little guy
I never thought about a rubber I always ran in them guts raw.
Sometimes I thought it was ludicrous
We fought every night I even called you a bitch.
You had so much potential but you drifted off into the mean streets
You loved me and I loved you but my mind was in defeat.
So the bond we shared was later deceased.
We use to say "Let death do us part"
But now you have to abrade away the love that's left on your heart
We have to depart.
Picasso drew up this love
And cupid took his arrow and tore this masterpiece apart.
Don't love me...

After all of this mayhem I thought my life was doomed
Sometimes I think I'm going to be single to the tomb.
Real love is rare.
Love Love Love
It's more potent than cocaine or any other form of drug
It will get you higher than any Dope or Percocet.
If you overdose on love you might as well embrace an early death
I tell people not to love me
And I tell people not to hug me.
That's the modesty in me.
I will have you bursting out of your shell like Shaq in a convertible buggie
I hope that you understand

Love, kisses, and hugs are the master disguise of a con man
Don't love me...

Loving you is the most beautiful bloodiest battle.
-Kondwani Fidel

    Confusion makes gaining knowledge very feasible. You have to understand why, how, and what confuses you and you will soon break loose from the ideas that have your mind puzzled. It's very interesting how there are many elements in life that we need to survive. It's also ironic how too much of anything can kill you; this world is such a contradiction.

Tangible Turmoil
You are my shackles, you are my freedom.
You are my epilepsy, you are my Caesar.
You are my maze, you are my blueprint.
You are my storm; you are my Noah's ship.

You are my water, you are my fire.
You are my Abe Lincoln, you are my liar.
You are my hatred, you are my desire.
You are my raw, you are my Whitney.
You are my Blackout, you are my Britney.

You are my breeze; you are something that's hard for me.
You are my number 1, you are my monogamy.
You are my stationary, you are my flight.
You are my blindside, you are my sight.
You are my heart, you are my soul.
You're the reason why my heart is ice cold.

> *Searching for love in a broken home*
> *is equivalent to searching for that one puff of smoke*
> *that gives a cigarette addict cancer.*
> *- Kondwani Fidel*

Right after I cried my first tears, cracked my first smile, and took my first breath I had been abandoned physically, mentally, and spiritually. My mother had me growing up thinking that maybe I am a cursed child. She had me thinking that I was caught up in my own pamper. She had me wondering "why doesn't my mother love me"? For many years she had me believing that it was something wrong with I. Whenever we get neglected or abandoned, it forces us to believe that we are Charlotte getting caught in our own web, when sometimes it is not our fault. No matter how big the obstacles are that you face in life, make sure you embrace them and then slay them with dignity.

Why Did You Leave Me?
Disappointment lies along the lines of abandonment.
Thinking that the people you love mean oh so something
Until they turn their back on you and leave you absolutely nothing.
So it forces you to do horrible things that are so disrupting
Then you lose yourself, so now your entire life you are Good Will Hunting.
So now you have to exercise caution,
While walking the treacherous streets of Boston.
Then you want to Jackie Robinson your dreams out of the ball park but you're only stuck to bunting.
Why is it that we will search our entire life for that something?
From an individual who left us with absolutely Nothing.

Times do get hard; we all know that's true.
But God doesn't station us
in battles that he can't help us pull through.
-Kondwani Fidel

As a youngin I always felt detained in a claustrophobic corner. Many times I would come home from elementary school and I would receive bad news from granny like "Mommy is gone" or "Mommy left for a while" or "Mommy made some bad decisions so the police came and took her away". The reason for her incarceration would vary between drug possession, assault, weapon charges, drug distribution, burglary, soliciting, trespassing, prostitution, sex offenses, theft, issuing false documents, forging documents, identity fraud, failures to appeal in court, and I'm sure there are many others. I would always wonder, how many bad decisions can one make? How much pain could a child like me take? These series of unfortunate events that went on for my entire life time involved my mother stealing from our home, her smoking coke, and sniffing blow right up under our noses. Emotionally, she distressed my grandmother, my younger siblings, and me. After the years went on I knew I had to leave very soon. I had to get away from this mayhem. The east side of Baltimore City was bad enough as it is, and on top of that my home was a wreck. God gives us blessings, and he also places us in obstacles. When you catch a glimpse of the slightest opportunity, embrace it and capture it; you have nothing to lose.

Trust the First Megabus
Once upon a time I lost feelings with my inner soul.
Cursed child that's lost in the world asking myself where did you go?
I slipped and tripped up
Never breaking, but sometimes I would fold
Always grasping on my thoughts that are destined for my goals.
When you smell a slight stench of an opportunity
Obliterate nonsense, and pay close attention with your eyes
The chicanery ways brought to you by peers will come in the most brilliant disguise.
So when you feel that your thoughts are scrambled,
Lost in the dust.
Trust your first instinct,
You will feel it in your gut.
Take your thoughts, inspirations, dreams, goals, and ambitions
And whip them all up into one pot in the kitchen.
Make sure you listen
Hear your soul speak
Overlook the fiction
Keep the distractions at a very far distance
So take that one pot that's filled with your desires and pack it up.
Love your desires
Kill the lust
And make sure you're the first to board the next Megabus.

Every idea that enters my brain turns me into a new person, therefore;
my character never repeats a day.
-Kondwani Fidel.

When someone calls themselves a "prophet" it captures people attention. The word is usually associated with someone who has supernatural characteristics, or someone who is sent by a God of some sort. So when people refer to themselves as prophets others look at it as blasphemous or crazy. Little do many know, prophecies are nothing more or less than speaking things into existence. I prophesize new things that I want to happen every single day. If you want anything in life you have to speak it first; you have to claim it in your mind before you actually possess it. Once you mentally claim it, then you are now in control of your thoughts. Now that you are in control of your thoughts, you are now in control of your actions. Therefore, everything you predicted is already done and placed into the universe. You see these things, however; everyone else is just waiting to get a glimpse.

Unsung Prophecy
Can anybody picture my prophecy? I'm gone in the wind
Can I bargain with God about how much time do I spend?
On this earth hurting, grieving with death I'm flirting
I am very alerting
It is not hard when your life is disconcerting
God knows my true worth but how much work am I inserting?
I'm on the outskirts of hell's home running around its surface
But I shine too bright for the devil he tried to pull down his curtains.
But it's not working,
There is a trigger in my mind and it is squeezing and bursting
It has enough bullets to put a hurting on a sergeant.
What's skeptical to me, how is there one God with so many different bible versions?
Follow me through my excursions and save your hateful aspersions.
People seen me down bad
I had to get up and get back.
I remember when I was last
I vividly remember my past
My mind is moving fast.
Just picture my prophecy; I want you all to be watching me.
Earth obstacles are obsolete; the stars mark the road for me.
Can anybody picture my prophecy and my predictions?
My vaticination is what you all are missing
People think they are so smart but their minds are locked in a prison.
Pick up a book that's where they hide the

unaccustomed info that will have us rightfully driven.
I'm not trying to portray an image like I have no flaws
So before all the vanity slaves get offended
Me I am no angel I sometimes fall victim.
Sometimes I bicker with my angels
And it leaves my soul dangling on many different angles.

> *If your friends and family don't
> force you to examine yourself
> and help you grow ... guess what?
> They don't have your best interest.*
> -Kondwani Fidel

Family is not only the relations that you have with the group of people you are born amongst. Family is a strong word that has more of a meaning to me that is much different than the norm. "Usually" your family consists of your parents, brothers, sisters, aunts, uncles, and grandparents. But in all actuality those people are not your family unless they show true love. Not just hugs and kisses but that love that bonds people together in a relationship that is unbreakable to any outsiders as well as other so called "family" that might try to damage and (or) break the chain. Family does not discriminate against color or race; Black, White, Hispanic, Korean, etc. A family stands alone and dies alone no matter the circumstances. If someone will fight blood, sweat, and tears for you and not think twice about it that is family. If all someone has left in their pocket is a bag of chips and one of your family members is hungry it shouldn't be a thought about not sharing. A family will take on the journey of going through the trenches and the jungle with another family member if it is needed. A family should not be afraid of failing just as much as they are not afraid of succeeding. When it all falls down a family has to survive together through any obstacle. It takes a strong family not too only keep the union they share with each other powerful and healthy. A strong family should as well build a dynasty for the family members coming along in the future.

Where is everyone?
My thoughts about my parents have embroiled me in controversy.
All I can recall is pain for years.
I even felt it in my embryo
The cocaine and the heroin mixed with Cheerio cereal.
I sit in a room hurting while it's filled with everybody.
Can you all believe the trick of vision?
Really I'm not in here with anybody.
Where is everyone?
My heart beats with confusion.
I thought I had friends.
I thought I had family
But it was all just an illusion.
Where did everyone go,
This injury broke the skin.

*It's ironic how a parent will tell their child
"Be careful in this house before
you break something"
when the home is already broken.
-Kondwani Fidel*

    Baltimore is that one place that will teach you the absolute right way to do all of the wrong things. Baltimore will make you so good at something that you will have no other choice to believe it is right because you are so good at it. The people here who sell drugs, steal cars, rob, etc. just might believe that those are the reason why they were put on Earth because they are masters at their craft.

Where I'm From
I arrived in a bloody cocaine wrapped placenta.
I was born but unborn.
Free but shackled
In this treacherous murder capital.
I was born in Baltimore's basement
In my imagination I had a spaceship.
But no righteous fuel or energy to fill the spaceship with.
We rape mother's Baltimore womb until our tombs,
Then leave it a bloody mess for the children.
Not so the children can clean it up, but to pick up where we left off.
For many years the pain we had slept off.
You would think the bright lights in Baltimore would be exciting to watch like a never before seen comet.
But when I step out into the streets filled with light
I walk into a zoo.
I get filled with darkness.

*Running away from your obstacles is like
jumping out of the way
of an imaginary sniper bullet.
Your moves are blank.
-Kondwani Fidel*

    True love is that one thing that many of us never really experienced or know the true meaning of. When you think of love, you think of happiness, pleasure, paradise, etc. When you recall situations when you were in love or thought you were in love, I'm sure you can recall many exceptional times as well as various fallacious times. Then you wonder how can something that's supposed to be so joyful hurt to this great of an extent? Why is something that's supposed to be so incredible bringing me so much pain? Love can be very exciting. Love can lead to much harm. Love can be very enticing. Love can also be a dirty game, so make sure you play it safe.

True Love
Love is so rare when do you know it's real?
True love is so rare how do you know what it feels?
Is true love real? Myself I forever ask
Watch out for hate when she's bearing and wearing love's mask.

Mike has a childlike heart and it's froze subzero or below
He just wanted to be her hero
And when the heat comes to be her Robert De Niro
Because he likes playing in her hair does that make him a weirdo?
Females don't realize the power they have
Her mind power control what's in between her legs.
Mike felt like he would do anything for this girl
He has not even traveled the globe and wants to give her the world.
Mike was totally in love, she made his heart feel milder.
Just to keep her company for one night he would take several showers
And scrub his butt and balls for a plethora of hours.
And every day he would send a text
Saying "Baby the world is OURS".
But she is running game
She ought to be ashamed
She think she is slicker than a can of oil,
On her Big Daddy Kane
She drained his heart
She drove this brother insane
Every other night she was calling him another dude name.
Mike was so passive he would act like nothing happened
In his alone time he would sit, mope, and cry about it.
He said to himself

"Her love I would die without it!!"
But she wasn't showing him any love
It was all a disguise
The kisses, sex, and the hugs.

Love is so rare when do you know it's real?
True love is so rare how do you know what it feels?
Is true love real? Myself I forever ask
Watch out for hate when she's bearing and wearing love's mask.

I forgot to mention
Mike's girl is in love
Not with him, but the kitchen
Not to make food but drugs are her addiction.
Cocaine and Heroin
She has no job so Mike gives her all of his bread
Not aware that he plays a large component to these sins.
Mike sits around and laugh broke as a joke
And say "the drugs make her happy I might as well sniff some coke"
Mike now enters into a fantasy world
And sees himself in love with a totally different girl.
A girl who loves him for him
Not one who tries to take him all in
Sleeping with other dudes
Thinking that it is cool
When really it is rude, low down dirty, and cruel.
This builds angry fuel
In Mike's heart
Mike is now thinking "I should have said forget this from the start"
So Mike keeps nodding and leaning
Rubbing his nose, he is feigning
He gets distracted by the devil on his shoulder screaming.
The devil said "Mike are you alright?

I know damn well you not gonna go through this all your life
Breaking up and making up for all this trife
Come on Mike, you have to be kidding
You are a very handsome young man you should be the one out here pimping.
But instead you are miserable, sniffing drugs and popping prescriptions
For a girl who talks all day but she don't listen
Ha-ha I know what will be fun
Go upstairs Mike,
You still got bullets in your gun
Go grab that forty five and bang at her torso until the cops come"
Mike is so gone off the drugs
He was easy influenced so he ran upstairs
He grabbed his gun and aimed it at her
He pulled the trigger screaming,
"You played me for a fool, hoe you drove me crazy.
No longer are you my lady.
And I be damned if I ever want you to have my baby"
Mike then looks at his trembling hand that holds a pistol.
Then he looks at his old girl.
Thinking, what did he do?
Damn it is a cold world.
You know Mike is very cowardly so he started crying a river
As soon as he simmered down he put 2 bullets in his own liver.
He took away his and her missssery
His last words "Bitch you will remember me"
He sat there for a while and started to shiver and quiver
Then he passed away
You can't play with a person's heart
Well at least that's what the pastors say.
Mike turned to the drugs for a little escape

And got distracted by the devil who crept down on his fate.
But hey, I just gotta say one thing.
Watch the minds and hearts you rape
It ain't no rules in this dirty game of love
Make sure you play it safe.

*Too much caring can simply hurt
one man.*
-Kondwani Fidel

There are many issues that we face in our everyday lives. Some of them we can change and some of them we cannot. If it something dealing with yourself, then of course you can change the situation you are in because of your decision making. When there are problems dealing with others that seem to affect you, there is nothing you can do but hope for the best. Throughout my life I would always stress out and beat myself up over the many problems that surrounded me. I had to realize that it is nothing that I can do but to keep moving forward with my own life and taking advantage of the opportunities that the universe put in my path.

Corrosive Care
I care about so many things I can't change
Wait, hold up let me explain
It's hard for me to maintain
The weather man said mad snow; all I see is good rain
My thoughts I try to reign
My thoughts are what make me go insane
I care so much about things I just can't change
It eats away at my heart
It eats away at my brain
Mother lost, Daddy lost.
Grandma is at her peak.
Grandma is weak.
She has been watching kids for more than 50 years,
She's drowning in stress.
She's been hit in the heart, the stress pierced through her
Bullet proof vest.

I care too much about things I can't change
Well at least change right now
I can change them one day but just not now
I'm trying to change things; I'm on a better route
I'm tired of stressing myself out.
Why must I care so much about things I can't change?
I'm deranged.

*Remember that you are extraordinary,
just like every other.*
-Kondwani Fidel

    Many women fail to realize that they all have different eyes, noses, faces, bodies, and skin colors for a reason. I don't believe that God made us individual people just so we can conform to someone else's will; which kills us slowly and we don't even know it. Many women die for a fantasy appearance, when they need reality to keep them alive. I'm not saying nothing is wrong with make-up but it should be used to compliment your beauty, not to trick the eyes of others about what you truly look like. I love all women, and I believe all women are beautiful in their own unique way without the use of materialistic illusions.

Destruction of Beauty
The one thing I deplore,
Is when beautiful females walk in heels
Stomping on their morals to be a pretend video whore.
Now a days, the true essence of beauty is watered down
And females wear so much make-up they look like tortured clowns.
Us men we gas them up
It keeps them masking up
Layer after layer after layer
They don't care that their natural look is the apple of a man's eye
They just keep on MAC-in up
Blush, lashes, mascara, and Sephora; they keep them stacking up
Some of you all drink fluids out of low esteem filled cups
Y'all just look in the mirror and say to y'all friends "girl look! Ain't my ass phattening up?"

It continues to bring the value of beauty down
I usually could smell beauty tiptoeing from around the corner, but now I can't hear a sound.
Wait,
Let me get it straight
Y'all pay hundreds of dollars for hair when you can grow it for free?
Am I tripping, is it me?
Whoever said Nappy or natural isn't the way to be?
Bundles of fake hair fill your bedtime scarf.
Then you lay your head on the pillow,
This snatches the illusion of beauty off.
My lovely ladies, please stop selling out
And conforming to being called cutie.
Can y'all please settle with my settlement and not try to sue me?

Can't you see this is nothing more than the
destruction of beauty?
I just want to show how much I appreciate all
You don't need make-up to emit light like the stars.
So stay how God made you in his original view
And forget the dudes who can't love you just for you.
This make-up to me is nothing but a disguise
So take it off so your real beauty can shone the torch
in my eyes.

Remember this is just my expression, I know
everything about truly nothing.
After reading this, will you look at me like the gadfly
bug?
I love all of my women
No matter how you choose to Picasso your body, who
am I to judge?
No matter what, all of my women I will forever love.

Sometimes you fill me with bewilderment.
Are you my sinful addiction?
-Kondwani Fidel

    I'm sure that many of my men in the world can testify to having a woman who is or has been a part of their life that brought them so much joy and brought them pain at the same time. No matter how much this woman betrays you and brings harm, you will still stick around and be in love. This is simply that one friend who you have to love at a distance because being too close might cause death.

Best I Never Had
Baby we had good times, baby we had bad.
But you gave me the best life I never had.
You gave me pleasure and you gave me pain.
You gave me sunshine and you gave me rain.
Baby I love you forever, I will never use your name in vein.
Forever my super woman never a Plain Jane.

Baby, remember all of the times you played me?
They said she was the murder capital and yea she killed a part of me.
She took me for granted and she damaged my heart
I knew her since I was young, training wheels from the start.
As years went on and on I became her counterpart.
She would send me on crazy missions, have me all tired
Everyone thought I would be a product of her environment.
But I dodged a bullet.
I left her for Virginia; I didn't mean to offend her.
I had to expand my knowledge, and take that clumsy trip to college.
She was a dirty shame and I still mingled with her
On several hot summer nights and blistering winters that was burr.
She had me skipping school, talking rude, and spending drug money on clothes, jewels, tattoos and fast food.
Every time I cut on the news she has killed somebody
She was a crazy girl and I kept her right by me.
She was putting the smack down on brothers like Scotty 2 Hotty
Because I was so attached to her, my grandmother started to deny me.
Granny said "you love that girl more than you love me, more than you love your life"

She taught me some strategies of how to maneuver through life.
She taught me how to spar with vultures during the days and nights.
Once upon a time she showed me that she loved me
Then I was in search just for someone to hug me
She was always a rough girl
Playing with her was like playing a Game of rugby
The lies, the truths, she couldn't even hug me
She showed me the good, the bad, the ugly

Baby we had good times, baby we had bad.
But you gave me the best life I never had.
You gave me pleasure and you gave me pain.
You gave me sunshine and you gave me rain.
Baby I love you forever, I will never will I use your name in vein.
Forever my super woman never a Plain Jane.

Once upon a time
She gave me Earth, Wind, and Fire
Before I could barely walk she took me much higher
Before Kanye West we've been through The Wire
This is more than what you seen on a HBO
But the biggest difference here is that this is not a TV show
She put coke in my mother's vision, and made her favorite smell blow
At many times she would make me gaze into her eyes.
Then I would look into the stars and see a riot in the sky.
Thunder storms and rain drops
We played in the rain until it stopped
We threw eggs and rocks at the cops
We ran through the city with no socks
She showed me my first glock
She handed me my first rocks
Orange, blue, red, green, and white tops

I love you baby, I love you baby
You will always set me free.
Baby I love you!
How could I ever forget thee?
But I know she could possibly forget me
What if she break my Nintendo? Then there is no more Wii
We will eventually reunite only time can see
When I think of two people loving, I never think we
Would she be happy with the man I am becoming?
Or will she keep dwelling in my past, and tapping on my old chamber door?
So just like Edgar Allan Poe
All I keep hearing is the black raven repeating nevermore.

She had me jumping in and out of stolen vehicles.
I always hated math but this girl,
This girl she was so strategical
Ahhhhhh them good memories why couldn't I stay with you?
Ahhhhhh them good memories why couldn't I have seen more?
My first real love
My heart I just poured
For eternity I will love my baby,
Baltimore.

> *Give me a reason as to why I should feel*
> *as special as you say I am?*
> *If you treat me the same as you*
> *treat another man.*
> *-Kondwani Fidel.*

Many of the relationships that I have been a part of play a role in my writings. The relationships vary from death, life, family, friends, and females that I have dealt with in the past or what I will deal with currently. Most of the work that is about these relationships is unconscious creativity. Since most of them are emotional, I would just throw my thoughts onto paper without much thought behind it. My writings are what I think, however, some of my pieces are inspired more by my feelings than thoughts.

My Last Duchess
That is a picture of my last duchess on my phone
smiling like she's still alive.
She always loved to smile at me.
But who passed her path and didn't receive almost
the same smile?

I never thought I could live without her
But it's no more we, because of the lies and how time
forever flies
I thought our relationship could forever rise
But our show got cancelled, no more televised
I want you and if I can't have you; no one else will
But I know you owe me nothing, put that in your will
It was all a big secret, no one ever peeped it.
My precious last duchess, what would people say to
us if they found out the truth, and had proof?
If we could ever possibly reunite again and conquer
with sins
I would make love to you forever
Show you off forever
Love you long forever
Never hurt you again never
Despite the trouble I put you through in the past or
whatever
This is my endeavor
If we became a force again, this love I would treasure
Now you can choose not to ever smile at me again,
Never.
Then I will make sure I stop all smiles all together.
I will make sure I release you from life clutches.
I will forever miss you
My last, my last, my last duchess.

No matter how hard something may be, if it has to get executed in order to benefit your life, then do it.
-Kondwani Fidel

    Sometimes when you look at past relationships that you have been in, you look back and see the time that you've invested has been wasted. In the moment you feel like you love the person, which may be true; at that particular moment. You then force yourself to be with a person for whatever reason, but sort of resent every minute of it. Until you reach that point when you know for certain you just can't portray the false idea of commitment because now this false idea is getting in the way of your real life success. During your journey towards success you have to get rid of some people in your life for you to progress and see the bigger picture that they are not a part of.

Freaky Dreams
I know I did some dirt, her record wasn't squeaky clean
She did a plethora of sneaky things
But all I can remember are the freaky things
And now the closest we get is when I have them freaky dreams.

Once upon a time I thought this girl was my soul mate
Never in a hundred years would I think she'd let my soul bake
I pitched her my heart, and she ran it all the way to home plate
You know how many months these smiles we faked?

We use to argue all day, all night long
Short conversations on the phone
Our love seemed it has outgrown
But the only thing we was prone, was to get drunk while drinking Manischewitz wine and Bacardi Lemon.
After, we would take off our masks then pack up
Then we would argue again, I'm thinking I knew I shouldn't commit.
One minute she claimed she loved me and my work; since I love her I plead the fifth.
Then she would get mad and say "Koni you and your poetry ain't shit"

After Valentine's Day, everything I purchased her she threw out.
And told me to get out.
Soon as I stepped foot, she would pout.

I know I did some dirt

But her record wasn't squeaky clean
I caught her texting other dudes
Doing a plethora of sneaky things.
She tried to hide it and she got caught slippin
My mind was scrambled, yea I was trippin.
So now I'm on a Mission
Impossible like Tom Cruise.
Trying to find a woman who cares about life more than her shoes.

I know I did some dirt, her record wasn't squeaky clean
She did a plethora of sneaky things
But all I can remember are the freaky things
And now the closest we get is when I have them freaky dreams.

She would always bring around this annoying friend, her name was Jenny Anne
I use to crack jokes on her because her head was shaped like a tittie man
And whenever I would get tipsy, because her mustache was thick like mine
I would slip up and call her Jimmy man.

As the days went along I took my mind off snooze
You know the saying; once you start searching you'll find clues
That will leave you confused and mentally abused
And when she got caught, she tried to flip the script and me she tried to accuse
Like a deceitful baby mother, placing a baby on a dude
That is not his, knowing he drinks nothing but Mountain Dews
She claimed she hated me for my lies like the Jews
As much as I wanted to blow up like Syria on the world news
I kept my composure,

But I was all on her back like scratches and tattoos
It took me to a much greater anger plateau
I gave her seven hundred and fifty seven curse words like I'm from Newport News
I can't lie, yea she left me bruised
I look back and think I should've picked a better choose
I should've checked her reviews
But I see I learn as I get older like Langston Hughes
Memories, love, fights, long nights
My mind is scrambled, what to do?
Time flies like an Albatross it's time to get Boozed.

I know I did some dirt, her record wasn't squeaky clean
She did a plethora of sneaky things
But all I can remember are the freaky things
And now the closest we get is when I have them freaky dreams.

Settling for accessibility can make your life really tough.
-Kondwani Fidel

There are many things that go on with females that we men would never understand. I was told by a friend that all females are not hoes and promiscuous because of choice. My rebuttal was fast and I explained to her how I believe that everyone has their own will power to do or not to do whatever they want. She then cut me off to say that, "sometimes it is just easier". It inspired me to write, it made the light bulb in my head catch fire. Then I thought to myself, she is a female and she would know. Also everyone knows that more people settle for easy because it requires little to no work. Nothing great is ever achieved in life without a struggle.

Easy Route
Who really wants to be that girl that nobody want?
She gives dudes her number,
But she doesn't really want them to call, it is all a front.
She is stern and stands firmly beside her morals
But her heart and her mind; sometimes they quarrel.
She will not give it up to any dude that looks good or that can cook good.

What girl urges to sit lonely in the corner because nobody wants her?
Her dreams of having a good guy get deferred
Because she wants to wait long years to meet her king
She doesn't settle for late night sex flings.
This good girl can no longer take the pressure of being "Good" anymore so she eventually gives in
And becomes loose like the rest of her women friends.
It's too hard to keep your legs closed and get the recognition you deserve
It's hard to have male friends while all of your girl friends have lovers,
While you're the one trying to keep your heart reserved.
It is hard when you feel like you're the loneliest person on Earth
Especially the females that get over looked because of their large girth.
It's hard when you are respectable of your body and soul.
Society and the media pressures you to be more sleazier
The moral of the story is
Some females think that being a hoe is a tad bit easier.

Taking it to the next level with a woman is like sticking your hand in a bag full of gold, on the chance of drawing out some copper.
-Kondwani Fidel

    I have dealt with a fair amount of woman in my lifetime. Some who stayed around longer than others; some who were smarter, prettier, and funnier than others. There are many females who share these qualities but one has never crossed my front yard that attains all of them. Many women that I came across in my lifetime lacked intelligence. Sometimes, more than often it wouldn't be lack of knowledge when it came to school/book work but actual common sense. Common sense is something that is not so common in the world. Intelligence is one key that I look for that really meets up to my standards. Not that I'm being snobbish, because I'm sure there are many people's standards that I would never make the cut for, whatever the reason may be. At the end of every day there is someone who is out there for you. If you look in the trashcan then you might have a good chance at pulling out garbage. If you search in the sky for a star, you might just get one.

I Yearn a Woman
I yearn a woman who's willing to go restless
To reveal her well-grounded love for me,
And stand firmly on da-feet.
I urge a woman to take my brain into custody,
And not just adopt and buckle my eyes
Sometimes the attire that can buckle your eyes,
Are the same tricks that creep up in a cripple disguise
You think they view you as a prize, but they really
despise and prey on your rapid demise.

I would be yanking my chain if I said
"I want a female to be my other half"
When you dudes say it, I'm sorry I don't comprehend
the math.
As to why us men want a woman who only has half?
And not her own whole
One who sweeps her own goals
One who promenades her own path
One who bathes in her own bath

I can admit, I'm frequently pessimistic.
But where are the women who are understanding?
Not so much demanding?
It's hard to find a GREAT woman whose body is
outstanding
While her mind is expanding.
Don't make me have to change myself to converse
with you
Or I'm going to have to disperse from you.

I ~~need~~ want a woman who will fight for me,
All night upright for me
If I point out a girl who was slick out to the mouth to
me
My woman would not ask one question
She is willing to smash someone on sight for me
If I write a bad poem, she will announce and try to re-

write for me
One who will display excite for me
One who won't show me the slightest of spite you see
Before you start saying "oh I feel he's right for me"
When the feelings are only slight to me
Remember you let me clap those cheeks on the first night for free?
So listen carefully as I say this politely
HOW DO YOU EVEN LIKE ME, WHEN YOU DONT EVEN KNOW.......
ME.

Appreciate every moment as you should
-Kondwani Fidel

    The word moment sounds so small and useless. Many moments are consciously and unconsciously unappreciated. I know that many of us have been told to enjoy our life and to have the best life as you possibly can, or something similar. People focus on living the greatest life ever, and they fail to do so. It's similar to building a brick house; you don't try to build the biggest house of all time. You focus on laying every brick as precise as a brick can be laid, and your end result will be a fantastic house. A great life time is made up of many great moments. On the other hand, the object of life is to have many astounding moments and then stack them together. Therefore, you enjoy every moment to the fullest extent, so then when you look at your life you will see the masterpiece which was built off of many extravagant moments.

The Minimal Moments
She said she feels like she's caught up in the moment
Only because I'm the moment she was missing
Although my previous motions is what she only remembers
That's when I was running the streets sleeping with several different women.
So when those thoughts entered her little brain
She started to drown away her troubled miseries and pain with light liquor
That tainted her liver
That crippled her character
Now whenever she talks she shakes and she shivers
Like Ali outside butt naked in a blizzard,
With the weather 30 below
Which made her heart turn cold
Like a winter wonderland in the break of December
So now the good moments and memories is all that I remember
I was always a firm believer of the prettiest people do the ugliest things.
So I use to say to myself "all pretty women are scary"
I put my pride to the side
He who looks the furthest has a vision that's blurry
I fell deeply in love for the first time only because God dared me
Now ironically I'm sitting here drinking, reading this obituary.

> *Love without fear.*
> *Love without doubt.*
> *Love without boundaries.*
> *-Kondwani Fidel*

When you are deeply in love with a person, no one will ever have to tell you how you and your significant other "should" act towards each other; nor the things you all should do together. Love has no limits, except the ones you create.

Bazaar
I know what I'm about write is bazaar
Don't judge me, and I hope I don't take this too far
Baby lets ride around in a stolen car,
With tinted windows so people can't tell who we are
But there's one catch
If we get caught, we might get stoned like Harold and Kumar.

I'll make sure not one stone hits your heart
If society approaches us, we will have to brawl
Because you know that I'm liable to snap like a bra
We shine during the day so people can't see that we're stars
The naked eyes can't distinguish your beauty, my Milky Way
Although you're forever down like the Southern Cross.
My thoughts barricade my brain, but you can't see the steel bars
I was told that even when you're up never put down your guards.
No matter how many blessings and struggles you receive never put down your God.

I use to never promote my potent poetry because people would say "boy you soft"
Now it's forget everybody I'm going off
My words are harder than a liar trying to plead troth.
These words are deep
For my certified freak.
Baby let's take it there
Don't ask me what, when, where?
I know what I wrote might sound kind of bazaar.
I know you're shy like a bulls fan
But baby can you be my Ride or Die?
For my unknown infinite life span?

> *Once you capture the mind of someone,*
> *you now are in full control of that person's*
> *entire being.*
> *-Kondwani Fidel*

Men are physical creatures and women are mental creatures. A woman is usually turned on by the mind state of a man. Women want a man who they can relate to mentally. If she lacks knowledge she does not want a guy who has more knowledge than her because they will not be able to relate during conversations and (or) when it comes to decision making amongst the two. She will want a guy who is on her level; therefore, she would rather for the conversations to be small instead of intellectual. If a woman is very intelligent, then a guy who lacks intelligence chances is very slim at getting this woman. This guy would not be able to relate to her mentally because he lacks knowledge. Now like I said men are physical. If a man sees a woman with banging body assets, that man will still want to indulge in sexual activities with her if she can't even pronounce her own name or barely say her ABC's. If every man is able to stimulate the mind of a woman, then I believe all men can have any woman that they desire.

Bum
If a guy could get any woman that he desires while wearing dirty baggy jeans,
Breath smells so horrible, that it makes Listerine flee the scene.
This guy is broke and dirty,
He doesn't have the tools to stunt
But contrary to popular belief, he can point at any girl in the world that he wants
And have them biting at his ankles, drooling all at once.

Now you have the flashy guy with the fresh Tims,
Jewels, with a fresh brim
A Breitling on his arm that shines brighter than lightning
He has fresh cars and fresh rims that sparkle like fresh gems
Do you get the picture I'm drawing?
There is this big shot guy that couldn't get a female if his life depended on it.
He says to himself "with women I can't win"
Now Mr. Flashy is pointing at the bum like
"Hey I wanna be just like him.
I'll take the baggy clothes, nasty breath, and the flaws.
And whatever else comes with the hobo all in all
Just for the attention of a woman and to get her draws"

A woman is the most highest prize of a man
They will do anything to get the ladies you understand.
If it attracts the woman, that is what the man is going to adapt to.
If the losers got all the women, wouldn't you want to lose too?

I remember seeing her once.
She was drop dead gorgeous.
-Kondwani Fidel

    No matter how gorgeous something is, never give it the benefit of the doubt. Danger does not have a favorite outfit; it can come disguised in any form, shape, or size. I have been hurt many times by people that I thought would never hurt a fly, and got bamboozled because I trusted that they wouldn't hurt. These many experiences were just valuable lessons teaching me that I had to get hurt in order to learn. In life you always get the lesson after the exam.

Autumn Crocus
The tyrant passion I have for this woman fills my heart with excitement.
The emotions are too intense.
This love forces me to do things unwillingly
I call her my...
She is the embodiment of hocus-pocus
She is one of the prettiest species I have ever seen and it is hard to focus.
The poisonous and toxic which the woman consists of is hidden beneath the bright shine that could burn you like a fluorescent light bulb.
She is a gorgeous majestic exquisite impression
She could make a snowman melt in the winter time.
How can something so beauty defying be so deadly and filled with danger?
It does nothing but make my blood boil and fill me with anger.
I guess its God playing tricks with my eyes
Letting me know that
The most vicious and deadly species come in the utmost magnificent disguise.

I'm learning to accept things
as they are and not what
I think they should be.
Although sometimes I feel
like the universe neglects thee.
When really all it does is test me.
-Kondwani Fidel

    Black is a color that represents elegance. It is a color that bleeds eminence and breathes power. Black is also an enigmatic color that is handcuffed and associated with fear, death, bad luck, and evil. Subconsciously many people ignore, steer clear of, and neglect the color black. While many people can't even give you a real reason as to why they do so. Giving black the cold shoulder is something that we all are, or have been guilty of. Like I said most of the time it's subconscious, and for others it is purposely done. It is sort of like rats being compared to squirrels. They both are rodents, they both carry diseases, and they both have similar looks (despite the tails and the complexion of their fur). A rat has never done anything to us but we have animosity towards them and cannot explain why we do not have the same animosity towards squirrels when they share the same attributes (ex: they both carry rabies). It's a tradition that is just passed down for years and years, with no true understanding as to why we share anger with rats. It's equivalent to how we pass down the "meaning" of black. Although the color black might represent darkness, it still shines like every other color.

The Black Jelly Bean
The black jelly beans
Fight by any means.
They always try to swindle to the peak of the bag,
Begging to get chosen
But get abandoned in the dark.
The black beans that are filled with jelly
Only reach the tongue, they never make it to the belly.

How about when you visit grandma's house,
And she has that jar filled with candy on the table during Easter.
The little jar contains a ton of jelly beans.
Everyone devours the beans, and then they go back
For a second round.
And if they make a mistake and pick up a black bean
They treat it as if fire was in their hand
And put it right back down.
The black beans are close to the others but yet so far.
It is now 5 Easters later and those same black jelly beans sit hopeless at the bottom of that same jar.

Just making it to the pit of a person's stomach
Not by mistake is all they dream.
Some people would rather die or drink gasoline
Before they eat the black jelly bean.

Our bleeding hearts frown,
while our bloody eyes falsely smirk.
-Kondwani Fidel

Every day you should try to tell someone something good about themselves. Tell them something that can better their day and enhance their mood. Find the time out of your day to talk to someone and help them get through their situation; you never know what a person is going through. Some people are blind and are still scared of the dark. Some people can see but are scared of what is in front of their faces. You could be the person to change their life just by talking to them.

I Ball
I cry when I am by my lonesome
I'm upset with the world that we dwell in today.
It seems everyone lives backwards.
Everyone has pseudo classic styles that mimic quintessential figures in society.
It seems like no one is different anymore, No one follows their own heart
Everyone wants to play someone else's part.
I cry because my heart is damaged
I cry because I grew up without either parent.
My silent cries become louder because no one feels my misery
No one takes the time out of their day to visit me.
To visit my energy
To visit my psyche
That twinges and birls at night
Although I'm filled with life,
I cry...I cry...I cry...I cry.
No one ever stops in this life that continues on forever
To take the time out and ask why does one cry
They would much rather carry on and pass by
It is agonizing and bitter, but sometimes more than often I would rather die
Then to sit around people while I'm balling and no one questions why.

I love the wisdom you shared.
You were there for me
Sometimes,
When no one else cared.
-Kondwani Fidel

    I am the Moss Rose because I bend with any storm. I grew up and was groomed into a young man who was born in bad soil. Through all of the dirt I maneuvered in, I emerged from it all with a few stains on my shirt. It's not about where I came from or how I got here; the beauty of it is that I survived.

Luzerne
This is where I lost my virginity
Where I took my first shot of Hennessy
This is where the ghost and most remember me.
I saw fights.
I lost battles.
I gained stripes.
I saw snakes rattle.
I smelled burning crack pipes.
During the summer time
I survived cold nights.

This world is a game, and we are all merely players
This world is merely a game, and we is the players
We is the game
We is the players
So play it right, before....
Before you play it
This block was a game
This block was my name
This block built me up
This block, it boxed me in
This block befriended me
This block changed, and foxed me again
This block had me feeling like nothing was ever the same
It changed on me
When I stayed the same homie.

They never taught us in school
The definition of The Golden Rule.
So here it is...
Get ready to write it down,
Follow me kids.
This world is a game, and we are merely players
We are nothing but flesh and bones with many sensitive layers.

The only thing tough as steel is steel
The only thing that is sharp as real is real.
But is real even real anymore?
When they burn down my block,
Will I be able to ride through the hood in my automobile
With my broken Achilles' heel?
I'll put it in this broke boy's will
After I kill my ego's ideal
Using this Pencil.

> *They will soon catch me and crucify me because of my five finger discounts.*
> *-Kondwani Fidel*

    What if you steal from someone who has an abundance of something? They have so much that after it is stolen they would not even know that something is missing. If you give it to someone else who is in dying need of it, is it really that bad?

The Hood Robin Hood
I'm The Hood Robin Hood.
I steal the knowledge from the rich and bring it back to the poor
I'm trying to get everyone to expand their intelligence more.
Many of us rob little Rodney just to pay pale Peter
Every little measurement of money, foot, inches, and millimeters.
Playing the little brown puppets
To them y'all are scrumptious, you Cousin Skeeters
Y'all own stomachs are empty
But y'all reach out your dirty spoons whenever they say "feed us"
Not realizing that you are cultivating the blue blood fetuses
Crave Leonardo Da Vinci's Italian ice for a little more than what you bargain for at Rita's
Can't y'all see that all we do is beat us?
We ignore the books cry for help
When they scream out "read us".
I'm sacrificing my life to give you all this knowledge
So please listen so you don't have to waste your time going to college
College is nothing more than the illusion of knowledge
Outside of the classroom is where your mind receives the most mileage.

> *Don't judge me off of what you heard.*
> *Not even all from what you seen.*
> *Judge me from all the obstacles*
> *I overcame.*
> *-Kondwani Fidel*

    We all have problems that we deal with; some more than others. I don't care how much a person acts like they are flawless and that they can't be touched. The devil does the same to all of his prey, just in different disguises. Some people keep their problems to themselves; some express them in their art and wear them on their sleeves. Not one soul on this Earth is perfect, no matter how much they put up a front. Everyone fights demons; some people lose and others win.

Couldn't Fathom A Title
Sitting around drinking Manischewitz,
Depressed, thinking what next.
I aced all of the devil's quizzes
But failed all of God's test
What did I do? Myself I suppressed
I hate to admit the truth but there is a first time for everything I guess.
I just keep thinking.
And it got me back to drinking,
And I keep sinking
My relationship with my friends just keep shrinking
My eyes get heavier as I keep blinking
After the last blink I slipped into a fantasy world.
I'm seeing double, I see myself under the table.
I'm juiced, I'm lit, so many thoughts
How do they fit?
I'm plastered, I'm crooked.
I'm liquored up, I feel shook.
I'm gone, I'm laced,
You can see it in my face.
I admit I need help.
Sometimes I don't want your helping hand.
It might cause me more harm and a lot more injury
As I drink away my pain I have thoughts about me dying
And I wonder will people remember me.

*Good decisions merely bring
the best results*
-Kondwani Fidel

    I have made many bad decisions in my life, from selling drugs to cheating on an exam in school to get a good grade so that I would not fail. Selling drugs was not a good decision, or was it really? I am not telling anyone that they should ever sell drugs because it is the wrong thing to do and it can lead you into a world of trouble. However, from selling drugs it was a good outcome for me at the time. This was during my sophomore and junior year of high school, where I attended Baltimore City College High. During the summer I would be out on the block which was right around the corner from my home. I would stand on these hot city streets selling heroin and cocaine to my fellow people who live in and outside of the community. While during the school year I would sell marijuana and food to my student body. I would sneak out of school during lunch time to the nearest McDonald's restaurant to purchase food, and sell it at double the price. I sold chips, cookies, juices, candy, etc. that I bought using my mother's food stamps before she sold them all. Although selling food was prohibited in school and selling drugs was prohibited by the law; I had my own money at the end of the day to provide my little brothers and grandmother with food, and sometimes I would even purchase her groceries and cigarettes. Although the things I did buy them was small, it gave me a feel of independence; knowing that my grandmother had to take care of my mother and my three younger siblings. Therefore; I felt like I was doing a good deed. I never had to sell drugs; it was something to do that was close to home and easy to get my hands on. It made me feel like I was doing something necessary, when really it was brainless of me because I could have did serious time in jail, got robbed, and (or) ended up being killed. Since I did not get caught, the outcome was good because it put me in a position to do many things such as helping my family. It also taught me a lesson of what not to do. Sometimes when I think about it, I say to myself "was it really a good idea"? I learned how to manage money, I became more independent, and I learned how to be more aware of my surroundings than before. What set me apart from many others was that I planned ahead how long I would do it, and how much money I wanted to make. I think that's what made the outcome good. Before you enter any game, mark your price before you enter. If it gets more expensive than the price you named in the beginning, then leave.

Bad Decisions
Bad decisions can bring suffering
Bad decisions can bring success.
Like cheating on an exam but you know that you will pass the test.
So is bad really bad?
Or is bad really good?
Females call themselves bad.
Are they misunderstood?
Good girls try to be bad and portray that they are from the hood
Which they are not accustomed, it serves them no good
So what makes a bad decision bad, the outcome or the actual decision?
Good or bad intentions just mark the outcome with precision.

Don't wonder if you already know the answer
-Kondwani Fidel

Life is merely a thing that is filled with many people who have thoughts of what the world should be, how people should act, and how people should love by comparing their life to others. In all actuality they should just try to live their own life instead of wondering what "should" be and to focus on how things are in their own life. The way someone loves will not be the same way that I love. Find what works out for you and stop comparing your life to others because you will find yourself trying to be someone else when we are all made individuals for a reason. That reason is to be our own person and not live by anyone else rules or expectations. Pick your own lifestyle and follow it because it suits you. Don't try to please or mimic others because you will end up in turmoil. Be the author of your own novel and be the hustler of your own ambitions.

Who Am I?
The life that we live in is filled with nothing but lies
People wonder how everyone knows their business, when their mouths are filled with nothing but eyes
Every master who becomes a master is filled with nothing but tries
Love is just a simple emotion that's captive in a chicanery disguise
Why is it we have the power to kill, without the power to die?
Who am I?
Just a Young artist giving you my point of view through my colorful eye.

> *Poetry is like magic, there is a certain feeling you get when you're real and you write, and people visit your psyche.*
> *-Kondwani Fidel*

The greatest joy an artist can achieve is the joy of when someone else understands their deep emotions that they release upon the world. Poetry is being free with no boundaries unless you place them on yourself. You break rules when it comes to poetry. What would art be if people did not break any rules? In this profession no one can tell you what to do, and if they try then they are doing nothing more than wasting their valuable breath. Poetry is my escape from the world that we live in. Many people call it "the real world" which I call "the fake world". Poetry is the real world, and that comes with imagination, which is something that many people lack. So therefore when I write, I become an adventurer who trundles around this world in search for the most complex or simplest of ideas and make them worth something.

Get Away
Believe in me like the stars up in the sky
How will you know your capabilities if you never try?
How would we enjoy life if no one ever died?
This lady told me once that I have a strong mind
What was ironic is that she was blind
Oh my, she must have felt my pain like it was written in braille
Who do I go to when everyone else fails?
I heard on y'all side that the grass is much greener
I cross the road and see that y'all chickens are much meaner.
The darkness levitates, while I try to mediate
I'm Sliding on thin ice telling myself "you better skate"
And fly higher than superman I guess I'll need a better cape
No kryptonite, all I need is a better cape.
I keep my mind running laps and that keeps me in better shape.
Like Tupac, I see death around the corner, come on don't hesitate.
When it finally comes, I pray that I'll be in a better place.
That's way beyond the 9 planets, trust me there's a better space.
They say to be early is to be on time so if I arrive 24 hours before my judgment day,
Do you think it will impress God so no longer I have to pay?
After reading this don't give me the "what's the matter face"
Darkness always real me in, temptation is her better bait
I'm going to get mine one day

Only God can truly dictate.
Some people call it karma.
Me I call it sudden fate
If I go to Hell I'm going to sneak into the sky
And pick the lock of Heaven's gate.

*Our lives might not have been
the party we wished for.
But while we are here
the least we could do is two-step*
-Kondwani Fidel

    Life is filled with many good and bad times. I've grown to appreciate my life more and more every day, instead of focusing on what I don't have. Never ignore what you don't have, but don't let it get into the way of your happiness and success. Focusing on all the wrong things in life can poison the fruits of your labor.

Good Life
Comparing my life now to my future has my mind in a loose not
Can I Lose? Not.
This Good life has been very good to me
Despite all the bad to the highest degree
Or the lowest debris.
I'm just trying to find a beautiful...
A beautiful world I'm trying to find.
Or is the life I'm living not beautiful enough?
I think so; everyday my eyes see beautiful women.
I can look up and see beautiful stars in the sky.
I can see my 2 grandmother's smile which can brighten up a dark cave.
My mother is still here after years and years of drug addiction and incarceration
If you knew the entire story you would be shocked she's still here tasting
This good life, oh how sometimes I take you for granted good life.
I graduated high school and I'm one of the few males in my family who went off to college, Isn't that beautiful?
I have 5 lovely little siblings who all look up to me, and one who looks down on me from Heaven's sky, isn't that quite nice
They have smiles which will brighten up any dark night.
The exquisite taste of Manischewitz I share with my tongue.
The beautiful breaths of air I breathe which fill my lungs.
A father who never gave me loot, but always gave me valuable lifelong lessons
To me that's a blessing.
I remember my father telling me "when you see chumps, ball your fist up"

I get high, I get high, I get high
Sometimes just thinking about this beautiful life
Why thank you good life, you are too kind
Why thank you good life, can this get any better with time?

Kill me now and my soul will live on forever
-Kondwani Fidel

Sometimes I think about how would life be if I could live forever. How would life be if I could be 20 years young forever? Would it be enjoyable? Would it be devastating? Would if we were all immortal?

Mortal immortal
I already live in a cold world I don't have to travel to La Brevine Switzerland
I want my soul to be free but many of you don't give a damn.
I want to be forever young,
God can you infinite my life span?
Would you rather die and miss out?
Live till your lungs give out?
Or be young forever
Live on forever
Witness life forever
Be wise forever
Having blinking eyes forever
A speaking tongue forever
Love and pain forever
Death will do us never
You and yourself together
That's all you'll have after 30,000 years
Watching life get better
Or maybe even worse
Life would be a casino rigged
You can spend time forever with millions of grand kids
And many of cousins,
Nephews and nieces,
Bundle of joys and pieces
That will soon be deceased and
That's the only problem about being forever young
Forever you'll see precious loathes of bread turn to wishful crumbs
All your life
Your eyes are being filled with years of death
Then you'll think living forever is getting old......
How can something get old to someone who's forever young?
What seems fun now won't be fun forever
The sun is sharp now, but that doesn't mean bright

skies forever
So would you rather live for eternity and not miss a beat?
And reach the highest peak
Finally death you can defeat

Or would you want to die whenever?
The next few seconds, minutes, hours, days, weeks, months, years, or decades
And have your soul just fade away at any day
You won't be able to witness every love one go to the grave
So would you rather be forever young, immortal?
Or someday have the reaper coming for you?

> *One can never sew a button onto*
> *their neighbor's mouth.*
> *Even if MaCaulay is Home Alone,*
> *they will find a way*
> *to raid the Culkin's house*
> *to see what they whisper about.*
> *-Kondwani Fidel*

    Many of us have a different terminology of what we call "our world" and the type of people who reside in it. I believe as an artist if you live in your own world then there will be three types of people who you come in contact with throughout your life time. The people who will enter your world because they share the same beliefs as you and you'll meet on a common ground. The people who think they believe in what you believe in, but they are falsely misguided and attracted to your beliefs for all the wrong reasons; therefore, these people will try to enter your world but will not be able to get in. Lastly, you will have those people who don't know too much about the actual world, their world, and let alone your world. So they will wonder around your home just falling through the cracks.

My World

People always try to find the world I'm in
My gin, my friends, my dough, and my sins
I'm about changing the world not following trends
I get envied by the men and school the women
I ain't got no Benz
All I got is a bike
People try to play me, but I'm not with the hike
I'm not with the hype
I always receive umber it is rare that I get light
Lay low for some days to come out in the night
All I do is speak my rhymes
So I don't lose my mind
So I can stay on my grind

Y'all take shots
It kills me when y'all want to know what world I'm in
My gin, my friends, my dough, and my sins
Y'all ask me crazy questions like y'all are informants
And then throw salt on me like y'all work for McCormick.
They ask me what are my career goals
I was told not to share them with anyone
So I said nothing.
Then got a nerve to ask me, who I'm humping?
They ask me what's cooling in my cup
They say "you know you are not supposed to be drinking, man that stuff gonna kill ya"
Manischewitz and Ciroc nothing gets realer.

I tell them that this is my life, this is my world.
I drink my own gin
I got different friends
I got low dough
And I commit sins
But at the end of the day I view life through a different lens
Nothing is guaranteed for tomorrow in this world I'm

in
My mind, heart, soul, and art
They all blend
The only thing that is guaranteed in this life of sin is
Earth's spin.

> *Just because a strong warrior lost a battle;*
> *it doesn't mean they didn't fight hard*
> *-Kondwani Fidel*

I'm not sure if there is a dictionary definition somewhere in the world that would reveal the meaning of my name, and I could care less what it actually said. My grandmother Gail said that she was browsing through a book that held African and Arabic names. She said she came across the name Kondwani, she liked the way it sounded and the meaning so she decided to name my father it who later named me after him. I was told by my grandmother that my name means "faithful warrior" and that is what I live by, stand on, and willing to die by. Every action and decision I make in my life, I always have faith no matter the outcome.

Can You See The Dignity In The Warrior?
Can you see the dignity in the warrior?
My father handed me his rusty tainted spear.
I got his murder weapon a little dirtier than it already was.
Then I doused it in good fortune by
Slaying every obstacle placed in my way.
If you look hard enough at this asperous artistry,
You can see that I'm knocking down
Barriers day by day.

Can you see the dignity in
The warrior?
He is fighting to start his own dynasty
Planting seeds to harvest his garden
Who cares that I was harvested in concrete?

Can you see the dignity in the warrior?
My flesh and spirit unify as one.
The warrior is breaking boundaries,
Harvesting with humility,
And growing twice as fast as those plants
Filled with simplicity.

> *I think ~~many~~ people ~~really~~ don't love ~~me~~.*
> *-Kondwani Fidel*

    I know for a fact that my art is not better than everyone else's. What I do know for a fact is that my art is different from everyone else's. I treasure my art how I do my life, and I treasure my life how I do my art. Although we are all made differently, no man should ever feel superior to the next. Love whatever it is you do, but love it with humility. If you don't have a great love for whatever it may be, a person or thing; then leave it alone for someone else to love.

Kondwani's Kreed

My heart is my companion, my heart is my art.
There are many hearts that love like mine
But do these other hearts love my art? Maybe in due time.
Sometimes it is there for me, sometimes it is not.
My hart is my life.
Trust me, I will master my hart before my black soul departs
From life's clumsy clutches that crutches
My hart is worthless without me, and I'm damn sure worthless without my hart
In order to survive this one of my many lives, I have to stay true to me and stay true to my hart.
I have to guard my hart and I have to shoot more precise at any and every one.
My words are like bullets that have been birthed from the hot sun
That will pierce lungs when they fire out this hot son of a gun.

Some will try to murder my hart
So therefore I have to dodge y'all darts
My hart tells me not to step on y'all targets like I'm managing Walmart.
My hart and I know what is accounted for in this wild treacherous war.
It's not the amount of art we create or the amount of noise we make.
Nor the minds we rape or the amount of words we let escape.
The only thing we will account for is the amount of masterpieces that strike the people's soul which makes it shake and levitate.
My art is animal, even as I.
My art is my heart, which is my life...
I will learn my art as I do my true brothers.
I will learn its impotence, and its units.

Random thought, but sometimes I get jealous of music.
I will learn its bells and whistles, its sights and its blind spots.
I will try to keep my hart taintless although my skin is tainted.
Before I die we will become one a part of each other.
Before God I swear this Kreed.
My hart defends my world and I defend my hart with no remorse on my sleeve.
We are the masters of our dream massacres.
We are the heroes of our own life.
In order to guard my body and soul from life's loud ass racket,
My lips will release fire that will guard my hart with a full metal jacket.
I am my hart and my hart is
Me.

*I constantly hear something knocking on my door.
I answer, just to find out that it is only fear and sin,
Throwing stones at my chamber saying "Koni bring your ass
back so we can kill your ass again"*
-Kondwani Fidel

When you think about geniuses, many of them were viewed as crazy. In order to be a genius you have to be overly obsessive about your craft. If someone is overly obsessive about their craft and they put that craft before their family, friends, and other duties they are responsible of, they will be looked at as bizarre and freakish. People who have passions are possessed by enthusiasm and excitement when it comes to their craft. I agree that does make us weird and a little strange. On the other hand; normal people do not have passions, they have passions and don't pursue them, or they have interest. Having a passion is different than having an interest. You can show your highest expression of talent by pursuing your passion. If you chase your interest you will only show mediocre abilities that can be performed by anyone. Your life will become a misadventure if you pursue your interest. If you have to go through 50 interests to then find your passion, make sure you do it. There is a very thin line between madness and genius; where do you fall into place?

Call me crazy
They say that I have bats in my belfry.
All I hear is people keep mentioning my name.
In negative ways
For days and days.
~~Family~~?
It's nothing but an Illusion.
They criticize me, ~~then they love me, then~~ they hate me.
The people who are my friends are my friends for life.
Or at least I think so
If poetry is crack, then I guess I'm the blow.
Or the modern day misunderstood Vincent Van Gogh
So is that why I KONnot hear anything?
Is that why during cold winters, I KONnot hear the spring?
I know nothing about nothing
So what do I really know?
Love? Talk that nonsense to the brainless scarecrow.
I'm crazy?
I have rats in my attic.
My thoughts are Jurassic
Which will make my work classic
Maybe my theories are drastic
If so, my drastic theories are what tie up my calligraphy tactics.
How does it feel to be trapped in your own traffic?
It's a feeling like using a stranger's chap stick
Sometimes the feeling is mutual even if it's your chap's stick
It Trumps up much tragic
But at least my philosophies are envisioning, while y'all philosophies are paper thin plastic.
I don't do drugs because I am drugs.
So I'm going to leave it to y'all to take my words and puff-puff pass it.
I would take a puff
But you know you can't get high on your own supply

You can't get blazed on your own J's.
All I hear is people keep mentioning my name,
When I see them they embrace me, yea they fake it
I know many didn't think this insane eager beaver bastard would make it.

> *My child hood I was scorn*
> *the doctors should've let me die*
> *when I was born.*
> *Now I'm cornered in an unpreventable storm.*
> *-Kondwani Fidel*

Don't ever go through life apologizing or feeling distraught about your struggles and (or) blessings the universe has handed you. God gives us challenges and blessings, so accept the bad just as willing as you would accept the good. The struggle has its gifts and curses, its ups and downs, and it has sunny days and bad weather. Through all of that, still find strength to stand up tall and to march up that road of happiness; it awaits you.

Ugly Memories

As I grow through life, I pray may the odds be ever in my favor.
Before my first fight I was screaming that I'm greater.
I know God is my savior,
No money for heaven's application
Because of my good deeds I will get my fee wavered.

We never believe anything stinks until we smell it,
So is that why Pandora opened the box that Zeus gave her with effortless ease?
When she was told not to, whatever that means.
And then what flew out of the box was every sickness and disease.
The only thing that was left in the box was some hope which was me.
One thing I can guarantee
Is that every last person who takes a read, will think back and agree
With every word that I spoke to the highest degree.
So to God, this is my plea.
To sweep up my past, every last bit of debris.
We all perform actions that might seem small or innocent.
Then end up dealing with extreme consequences.
Growing up in Baltimore, dreams were illegal around here.
They tried to tell me not to fly my dreams, because they will get shot with desert eagles around here.
Poetry needed some resurrection.
So God sent me some blessings.
And told me to be the alarm clock to wake the universe up from resting.
But no matter how far I climb the ladder, how much I increase my levels.
No matter how many steps I take they still make it their business to remind me I'm from the ghetto.

Memories are beautiful
Memories can be ugly
Sometimes I ask my memories, why didn't you love me?
Memories, oh memories they brought much sorrow
But all I can do now is root for a better tomorrow.

I witnessed my 8 year old little brother burn up in flames.
While the fire fighters carry him out the front window of his home and all you seen was his guts and his brains.
As much as I try not to envision this tragedy, it has been 9 years and the memory still lingers on My brain which drives me insane.
He didn't have many cards dealt
He was only in the 3rd grade.
They say the Good die young, but this I couldn't fade.
So what we have different mothers
Nothing changes the fact of you being my little brother.
I remember we use to laugh, play fight, and talk trash.
And whenever I talk about this story it feels like I'm chewing on glass.
All of our good memories will forever remain.
I just wish that I could see you again.
We have to learn that we are all puppets and the universe is Geppetto
The bright side is you was the first one to make it up out the ghetto.
I ask God all the time, why couldn't your life be further drawn.
Although you gone I gotta stay strong
All I have for your memories are distorted ashes,
God Please help me get past this.

Memories are beautiful.
Memories can be ugly.

Sometimes I ask my memories, why didn't you love me?
Memories, oh memories they brought much sorrow.
But all I can do now is root for a better tomorrow.

My teething ring was numbed with madness
And filled with nothing but sadness.
No man is free from sin.
I had it bad growing up, for new parents I use to recommend.
Because when my father was blazed off heroin and plastered off gin,
He would lurk late nights or broad day, and pull out guns to rob my own friends.

MEMORIES!!!!
I remember these memories just like that.
Laying on the living room floor watching Hey Arnold and Rug Rats.
6 deep the police came and burst through the back.
Fully equipped and strapped with black gats.
It had to be bad luck because I was the young black cat.
People use to wonder how could a boy get straight A's like the Braves.
When every other week his house was experiencing a police raid.

My mother burned pieces of my heart,
And these missing pieces is what reflect on my art.
Like the stars coming out in the afternoon on a summer day a quarter pas one,
That's how, that's how she violated her son.
I would always receive bad news like the 7.5.7.
Sometimes I wish I was a still born I could've just went straight to Heaven.
And dodged all of these bullets that pierced my little lungs, from these 2 son of a guns.

All I want do is relive my child hood and have some real fun!!!!!

I don't need confusing metaphors and similes to paint you all my extremities.
I just ask that when I die....
That you all remember me.

I remember my grandmother bought me a bike on my 13th birthday.
My mother then stole and sold it the next day.
So she can go buy some drugs from Ray Ray.
If I could just steal one wish from Ray Jay.
It would be to spend a Christmas with my both of my parents like Craig and Day Day.
No Friday After Next!
But I remember on Easter Sunday, I was nearly grazed by a bullet
From the victims my father robbed right in front of my steps.

Nothing I'm speaking is made up.
Yes I came up rough.
Nothing I construct in my art is to make me look tough.
I might have a little frame but my mind is too buff.
My head is only but so big how can it fit all this stuff?
My mother would harass my grandmother for money so she could buy blow.
Whenever granny said, "me no hablo, no good bye go"
It would lead to cold nights like Chicago.
Because my mother would then bust out all of our windows.
And she is the reason that today while my granny is dying slow.
I'm sorry I can't fathom any more
I gotta go.

In counting, last month would have made 8 months that my mother has been cleaned.
But don't get excited just yet, you'll comprehend what I mean.
I said last month because now
She turned back to fiend.
Back to a junkie willing to get high by any means.
She left my little siblings abandoned.
In the trenches of Baltimore stranded.
My little dogs were too young to know about Ques, but she left their hearts branded.
You don't need a pencil or pen to construct this sort of math.
When All I'm trying to say is,
I just want to relive my childhood with my mom and my dad.

Just like Sophia, All my life I had to fight!
A boy child is not safe in a family that's filled with spite.
The struggles I faced as a child is what help me now to maintain.
So I will fight till the death, until I'm the lone victor who remains.
So that's why I volunteered tribute to this life what I call The Hunger Games.
I was born into a war and I've been brawling in this bad weather but naked with nothing but my soul and my name.
The forecast in my world was cloudy, but from now on until the day I die
You all will forever see my reign.

I'm just waiting to be placed with my troubled crown.

"Rest in Peace Fidel Russell and Raysharde Sinclair.
You two will live forever."

Made in the USA
Middletown, DE
02 October 2015